FIX UNEMPLOYMENT, AND THIS WILL FIX THE MARKET: A 21st Century Solution

By

Jim Green

DEDICATED TO:

To those seeking to make the world a better place....

ISBN-10: 1511895187

ISBN-13: 978-1511895187

PROLOGUE

86% OF AMERICANS believe that "anybody wanting to work, should be able to find a job"--and yet, few know that we have the "legal authorization", on the books [15 U.S. Code § 3101] to limit our UR to "3%"--permanently......

And the model for our job creation in America, today—and since WW II—has been "Fix the market, and this will fix unemployment", rather than "Fix unemployment, and this will fix the market".....with the result of our being 180 degrees off *course—A Disaster*.....

In the very narrow window at the beginning of the Obama administration, when the senate, house and presidency were held by Democrats—we had the opportunity to make the permanent fix to our economy, above--but inexplicably they continued on the anachronistic, and unworkable path "Fix the market, and this will fix unemployment" [HR 2847]--and in spite of the electorate's mantra in 2008, before the *meltdown—FIX UNEMPLOYMENT*

And when the Democrats failed to do that—as we inched down at a snail's pace from 10% --a retaliatory electorate filled the House with lunatics in the 2010 election—and being a census year, the newly elected Republicans gerrymandered districts and thus guaranteed Washington will be in gridlock until at least 2020...A DISASTER, by definition.....

And in the 2012 election, we had the lowest turn out since the 1950's, and gave the majority of the Senate to the Republicans—and even less chance to fix unemployment in America......

We are a democracy—so why isn't the law, above, being enforced...why isn't the 3% a fact, and why isn't Washington listening to the American people?

The over-arching reason, of course, is because we don't vote [more later]—and while we slept in, the oligarchy took over, i.e., we have allowed the special interests to call the shots—less clear is that we have been duped.....

For instance, most Americans believe that "the market can provide anybody wanting a job, with a job"--and this has been our sole job creation methodology, at the behest of the oligarchy, since WW II—and yet, it is a *false* belief.

In fact, *only once* since WW II has this resulted in a

UER below 3%--in 1953—leaving millions jobless in its wake and indifferent to the pernicious consequences of unemployment, both for the individual and the larger society—i.e.,to the detriment of *everyone,* including the *market* [more on this latter point, shortly]....

Here are some basics...[all numbers approximate] every year 4 million children are born in America [a number that gets larger every year]--and when factored down this translates into the necessity that we create 200, 000 jobs every month just to keep up with the birthrate.

So when we see fewer jobs than that being created every month, it means we are falling behind—or if we subtract the 200,000 from the number of jobs created per the monthly DOL report—this number is the true number of jobs created that month.

It is little wonder why the Democrats celebrate the positive side of this picture—as we inch toward recovery—given the vitriolic climate in Washington—but given "automation", alone, fewer and fewer jobs are being created the further we advance into the 21st Century—and unless, or until we start enforcing the "legal authorization" [hereafter LEA], in 15 U.S. Code § 3101, above--our UER will grow exponentially going forward.

And yet, we have but a lone member of Congress

seeking to enforce this LEA—Congressman Conyers—HR 1000, a Bill which died in Committee at the close of the 113th Congress.

And while HR 1000 gets to the same place in reducing our UER to 3%, here is my solution for how we can end our unemployment crisis, tomorrow:

Incidentally, both are Pro-Market, and deficit-neutral—specifically THE NEIGHBOR-TO-NEIGHBOR JOB CREATION ACT [hereafter NTN]: a federally mandated, Social Insurance, owned by our employed [if one works, they would pay in]--to provide a fund to hire/train our unemployed.

For a modest 4% of salary policy cost, we could reduce our UER to 3% within six months of passage, and this methodology will create more "private-sector" jobs in six months, than our current method [HR 2847] in six years!

Jobs beget jobs....and the reality is that we have far more work that needs to be done in America, than we have persons to fill these jobs—*and under NTN grants would be made to local jurisdictions* [and the propaganda about "make work" jobs is nonsense].

A temporary large federal workforce, such as WPA, as an interim step until the market recovers--

doesn't work in our 21st Century economy—and particularly when an expanding and contracting public workforce, *with renewable funding*, is *indispensable* to the *effectively* functioning of a modern market economy—and triggered anytime our UER drops below 3%.

See also, The Buffer Stock Employment Model—with the public workforce expanding during downturns in the market, and contracting as employees return to the private-sector [triggered at 3% under our law--15 U.S. Code § 3101].

This is a Pro-Market solution....

Up to now, the path we have been on is "Fix the market, and this will fix unemployment"--[it doesn't work, today—the results are the proof]--and the exact opposite is essential in our current Zeitgeist-- "Fix unemployment, and this will fix the market".

To bring about this change, however, we need to take a hard look at our current system, and how we got here....

Since WW II the 1%--and the Koch brothers in particular, have spent hundreds of millions of dollars buying governors and legislatures to destroy our labor unions, and cement "at will" employment in every state [only Montana limits "at will" to probationary employees]--and the harsh reality is that for many in the 1%, American "employees" are looked upon as a POOL OF SLAVES: To Be Used and Discarded "at will" [Amazon/Kindle]....i.e., in the name of pure GREED, [and to relegate America to the 14th Century when we had kings and serfs]--i.e., they want persons without rights—a slave by definition.

The bright side of this very dark scenario is that a few, not enough unfortunately, are beginning to see that putting the rights of employees, last, or non-existent—is cutting into their profits—and while the examples are rare, a small company, this past week, decided to raise the minimum wage for their 120 staff to $70,000 per year, and the average employee wage at Costco is $21.00 per hour.

And while a salary increase is meaningless to a person who is unemployed—*the point is the trend*---and there are solid reasons for change.

We have two choices going forward—adapt and change in a world that is changing whether we like it or not, or create a Police State to hold our anachronistic laws and policies in place, and sadly America, to date, has chosen the later—and Ferguson, to name only one, is the result.....

And, unemployment is a *No One Wins*—the jobless lose, civility loses, and the market loses, to wit:

THE LAW OF DIMINISHED INCOME TO THE MARKET FROM UNEMPLOYMENT [hereafter the D/UE LAW]

3% is the zero-sum threshold above which unemployment triggers inflation by diminishing labor training and skills, under-utilizing capital resources, reducing the rate of productivity advance, increasing unit labor costs, reducing the general supply of goods and services--and the loss in income to the Market is compounded exponentially with each percentage point of increase in unemployment, above 3%.

Short Definition:

3% is the zero-sum threshold above which unemployment starts substantially undermining the Market--and the loss in income to the Market is compounded exponentially with each percentage point of increase in unemployment, above 3%.

Here is the reality: We have lost over 60,000 manufacturing facilities in the U.S. since 2000, taking millions of American jobs with them—and while it is obvious that many were lost because the windfall of cash Bush/Republicans gave to the 1%, in tax cuts, was used to build factories in the Far

East [with hidden profits in the Cayman Islands]--but the other reality is that people do not buy the products made in America, when they are jobless...

And the cruel joke being peddled to the American people is the propaganda that "the market can provide anybody wanting a job, with a job"--it is a flat out lie....

Among other things, every waking moment in capitalism is spent pondering how to eliminate jobs--to increase profits--not create jobs....even disregarding the erratic nature of the market—under any rational scheme, the last place we should look for job creation—is the market....

So, there is our road map for how to end our unemployment crisis, tomorrow--IMHO--but the lynchpin in all of this is to end our war against "public-sector" jobs—both in Washington, and elsewhere--they are _critical_ to the _effective_ functioning of capitalism in our 21Century market economy.

A few closing comments in the Prologue—an entire book could be dedicated to voting, in a "democracy"—indeed, given the make-up of the current Republican controlled Congress—it gets down right scary. Studies show that we vote more on "emotion", than human intelligence—and to show how far we can be from getting it right—aside from the Republican Congress—millions of Germans voted for Hitler—until he turned Germany into a dictatorship!

And while not ignoring how negative political ads turn American voters off—i.e, and they don't vote—we need to be keenly aware of how pernicious *propaganda* influences those who do—i.e., FAUX, the Tea Party—it doesn't bode well for America's survival.....and how can we forget that in 1925, when England declared a holiday—one out of four humans on Earth, took the day off—by 1975, it was England who? And all the warning signs are there—Citizens United [among others]—when the SCUS put our governance up for sale to the highest bidder...the warning signs ahead say "Fall", as in the Roman Empire—But I preach to the choir...but also, hopefully we agree we can turn this around--if our *informed, really informed--VOTE!*

Incidentally, I published my first book on my 78th birthday—and not that I write that fast, or well—the materials were all there for the better part of the past 30 years, give or take, gathering dust—it was just a matter of pulling them together in some order—also, don't believe any book should be over 60 pages, plus/minus-- i.e., can be read in the crapper--two hours, max--lol—but it seems best summed up by a very astute observer [wish I could recall their name to give credit]: Persons who write do so because they have no choice [it is a compulsion, an addiction..]—they become an "author", however, when people start reading what they have written....

Also, my favorite quote is from Oscar Wilde who averred "The only truly worthless opinion is an unbiased one"—so bias, agreed—but always in the interest in getting at the larger goal—the truth....

Finally, a note to the reader—the chapters that follow are intended to expand on the above....hopefully to shed more light—mostly in letters to President Obama/The Council of Economic Advisers---the papers and letters are not in sequence, and apologize for redundancy [please look for the nuance and nuggets...Thx--]—

Also, if you are a "typo-wonk"—are more concerned with sentence structure, etc., than content—you probably won't like my writing—and you will find a wayward capital letter, here and there, and appearing out of place and used for emphasis—I chalk up to editorial license and tongue-in-cheek, self-effacing humor—so apologies, here—[I seriously support: Take what you do seriously, but never yourself...for instance, the title, here, is both tongue-in-cheek, and dead serious]....

Just look for content, please....THX

CHAPTER ONE

President Obama/Council of Economic Advisers:

Since WW II we have had two parallel paths for job creation in America, and in many respects they are at war with each other:

One, path [A], seeks the full employment of Americans. The goal of the other [B], has been to crush the rights of American employees, and our labor unions—with little or no regard for the pernicious consequences of this goal--

In 1946, President Truman signed into law the [Full] Employment Act of 1946—to provide work for our returning troops—but, to counter this , B started the propaganda fraud that "the market can provide anybody wanting a job, with a job"--to undermine this law.

And based on this fraud, virtually every Republican in Congress [to this day], believes—really believes—and state it as "fact" [this is what makes it a fraud]--in spite of the facts showing this to be a myth—a belief, incidentally, much like our climate deniers [is indifferent to facts]....

In fact, under plan B [our sole method of job creation since WW II]--only *ONCE* has this resulted in a UE rate below 3%--in 1953—leaving millions jobless in its wake—and yet, it is the Republicans One and Only job creation program—to this day! Further under plan B—if the market fails, the jobless are out of luck....

Getting back to our parallel paths—in the mid-1970's the world economy underwent a major paradigm shift due to the colliding forces of automation, technology, globalization, etc., reaching critical mass—and "High and persistent unemployment has pervaded almost every OECD country since the mid-1970's.", Dr. William F. Mitchell.

As a direct result of this economic shift, America sprung into action--and in 1978, President Carter signed into law the most important legislation in the 20th Century—the authors, one white, one black—one a former vice-president—the law provides us with the "legal authorization" to limit our UE rate in America, to "3%", permanently.

The law infuriated B, in spite of it being Pro-Market [plethoric GREED does not fully explain—the Koch brothers, et al....also want to return America to the 14th Century—when we had kings and serfs....], and since WW II, the proponents of B have spent hundreds of millions buying legislators and governors, to cement "at will" employment in America [only Montana limits to probation], and to decimate our labor unions—the most recent assault on March 9, 2015, via Walker.

Solution: deficit-neutral HR 1000, and/or "The Neighbor-To-Neighbor Job Creation Act", Amazon

Jim Green, Democrat opponent to Lamar Smith, 2000

CHAPTER TWO

Fareed Zakaria/your guest James Baker 4/5/15

NEVER TRUST A REPUBLICAN.....

The Koch brothers, a metaphor, here, for the Plutocracy/Oligarchy [hereafter P/O] say trust us....cut our taxes and we will do right by the American people in building a good and decent society—

But look at their deeds.....as just one example, they want to destroy Social Security Insurance....indeed, their mouthpiece, the Republican party has tried to destroy Social Security from day one, since it became law in 1935....and yet the program has never cost the P/O a dime [they pass their cost along in the cost of consumer goods]--and it has improved the lives of millions of Americans—

In short, Social Security Insurance is *indispensable* is in building a good and decent society!

Further, President Obama had a weapon not available to FDR, after the Republicans, and Bush II in particular trashed our economy—the $800 plus billions in Social Security Insurance claims percolating up through our economy after the 2008 meltdown...that is, but for these moneys we would not be talking about having narrowly averted another Great Depression—we would be buried in one!

The truth is the P/O don't want to pay any taxes—and are opposed to a blended economy advocated by Democrats—but the reality is that save for the $2.7 trillion plus infused back into our economy, annually, by the federal government--capitalism in America would fold in a New York Second!

Finally, A good example for why we should never trust a Republican, who don't want to pay any taxes—all we need do is look at India—where they don't have any taxes. It has resulted in a caste system—with extreme rich and extreme poverty—and while India is purported to be in transition, it is hardly a model for building a good and decent society.

Ref: FULL EMPLOYMENT IS A PRO-MARKET CONCEPT, Amazon/Kindle

Jim Green, Democrat opponent to Lamar Smith, Congress, 2000

CHAPTER THREE

THE HISTORY OF HOW WE GOT WHERE WE ARE
[WW II to Present]

Following WW II, President Truman signed into law the [FULL] EMPLOYMENT ACT of 1946, to provide employment for our returning troops.

Ironically, half-way around the world, Australia codified into their law an almost identical Bill, and for the same reason—

Difference is—Australia actually put their law into effect, and over the next 30 years it was intrinsic to employment policy in Australia that "anybody wanting to work should be able to find a job"—and save for a brief recession in 1961/62 their unemployment was 2%, or less. This period is still referred to as their "Golden Age", in Australia.

Unforeseen by either country, however, in the mid-1970's the world economy underwent a major paradigm shift as a result of the colliding forces of automation, globalization, technology, etc., reaching a critical mass—in brief, an adjustment towards modernity—From a perverse perspective, we became victims of our success....

The instability caused by this transition, however, resulted in a malaise, and ushered in the ill-winds of greed-driven neo-liberalism with its indifference to unemployment, and the likes of Thatcher and Reagan—and the menace of this greed-driven agenda was exploded by Bush II, resulting in obscene disparities in wealth that persists, and is the cause of much friction between right and left, to this day.

It also ushered in high and pervasive unemployment throughout our market-driven economies, the OECD—with 6% unemployment in Australia now the norm, and double-digit unemployment common throughout the Eurozone, to this day.

As a result of the "malaise", however, the U.S. took an aggressive, pro-active role in addressing the, above, economic shift—and in 1978 President Carter signed into law one of the most important laws in the 20th Century--an expansion of President Truman's full employment, i.e., Pro-Market 15 USC § 3101--which provides a *legal authorization*" to create a "reservoir of public employees" [*indispensable to the effective functioning of a 21st Century market economy*]--at any time our unemployment in America exceeds "3%"—

But in spite of 3% unemployment being the threshold point above which unemployment starts substantially undermining the Market—this _legal authorization_ has never been implemented--

And in spite of deficit-neutral HR 1000, or The Neighbor-To-Neighbor Job Creation Act—A federally mandated Social Insurance, owned by our employed, to provide a fund to hire/train our unemployed—[more on the critical need to apply this job creation methodology in a 21st Century market economy, ahead]….

Ref: FULL EMPLOYMENT IS A PRO-MARKET CONCEPT, Amazon/Kindle

Jim Green, Democrat opponent to Lamar Smith, Congress, 2000

CHAPTER FOUR

THE HISTORY OF HOW WE GOT WHERE WE ARE
[Mid-1970's to Present]

In the mid-1970's, the colliding forces of automation, technology, globalization, etc., reached a critical mass—resulting in a Market no longer capable of producing the jobs necessary to its viability, and causing ubiquitous unemployment in all of the OECD countries—and leaving their leaders conflicted, ever since, regarding the displaced employee. Eurozone unemployment is still in double digits, and Greece and Spain both in excess of 20%, plus. High unemployment was also a major factor in Arab Spring.

In the U.S., we took a pro-active role in addressing this economic shift—and in 1978 President Carter signed into law 15 USC § 3101--which "authorizes" the creation of a "reservoir of public employment" at any time our unemployment in America exceeds "3%".

In 1979, however, and in a panic over Humphrey-Hawkins—our ultra-conservative foundations, and desperate to promote the Supply-Side fraud, embraced a flawed paper by an obscure MIT student, David L. Birch "The Job Generation Process"; and [with lots of cash] gave his paper biblical importance, and every president since has cited his finding as gospel.

Birch's paper concluded that "small businesses" were the greatest generator of new jobs—problem is, for the purposes of policy-making—it is BS. In a study at Harvard University in 2010, "The Myth of Small Business Job Creation" The research shows "no systematic relationship between firm size and growth." And that small businesses can actually detract from job growth.

In spite of this, however, Washington struggles, still, to make this antiquated notion, work--that it is only the market that can create jobs—and the result has been a disaster, politically as well as otherwise!

It would be impossible to still have 5.5% unemployment—if we were on the right path—and among other problems with this concept--if the market fails, the unemployed are out of luck.

Further, unemployment is a "social" problem—we as the larger society have an absolute responsibility to address—and yet, we are seeking to address with a highly unstable, incompatible entity: The Market

What apparently isn't clear going forward is that an expanding and contracting public workforce is an *indispensable* component to the *effective* functioning of a modern market economy—

The market thrives when we have a robust, employed, consuming workforce—and overlooked is that HR 1000 [currently in Committee], and the proposed "Neighbor-To-Neighbor Job Creation Act" www.Inclusivism.org [both authorized under Humphrey-Hawkins], are deficit-neutral--Pro-Market "win-win" solutions:

The American people win, and capitalism wins—

Jim Green, Democrat candidate for Congress, 2000

CHAPTER FIVE

President Obama/Council of Economic Advisers:

Capitalism is ideal in producing and selling corn flakes and cars—It doesn't work in solving "social problems" such as unemployment and our healthcare....

And when we have tried "privatization" to solve our social problems—it has been a disaster:

Essential programs have been cut—such as the elimination of text books from the Job Corps education program—to increase profits, and cronyism has run rampant—

And in our "for profit" healthcare system, billions of dollars are siphoned away from the premiums we send in—and do not go to the healthcare of ANYONE—but rather is used to pay for lobbyists, to make the CEO's filthy rich—and spent on propaganda ads to keep it that way!

Further, it attracts a few who see healthcare as a means to get rich, rather than cure the ill....

The truth is, we currently have a blended system—and they are, in fact, indispensable to each other:

Were it not for Social Security Insurance moneys percolating up through our economy in 2008—we would not be talking about having narrowly averted another Great Depression—We would be buried in one!

Social Insurance is a vital ingredient in building a vibrant and decent society—And, invent a better widget, sell the company for a million bucks, and retire in South Florida [capitalism]—is as well a vital ingredient in building a vibrant and decent society.

So why do we have this war of words pitting the two against each other—rather than educating the American people regarding the indispensable symbiotic relationship they have to each other?

Were it not for the $2 trillion + Washington infuses into the economy annually—capitalism would fold in a NY Second!

And yet, most Republicans ask God in their prayers at night to be protected from becoming communists, or socialists, or even worse "liberals"—i.e., ignorant of what the terms mean.....

And this war of words disguises that the Republican Party, today, is not the Pro-Market party they boast—but rather their policies are, in fact, Anti-Market—destructive to capitalism!

Pandering to the GREED of their wealthiest contributors—the Republican One and Only program—is NOT a Pro-Market concept!

Another misnomer in the war of words, is right-wing invented "entitlement"—a word that should be banned from honest discussion—do we refer to our auto insurance as an "entitlement"?

And when Social Security Insurance brings in more that it pays out, i.e., is deficit-neutral--how is that an "entitlement", and why is it portrayed in our graphs as a "government expense"—or even included in these graphs? If a corporation reported a massive loss on a product they in fact made money—they would be charged with fraud in a

New York Minute!

The list goes on—please see: OUR GREED AND IGNORANCE, on Amazon/Kindle

Jim Green, Democrat congressional opponent to Lamar Smith, 2000

CHAPTER SIX

President Obama/Council of Economic Advisers:

WHEN ON EARTH IS SOMEONE GOING TO TELL THE TRUTH ABOUT THE REPUBLICAN PARTY, TODAY?

The Republican's method of "job creation" being peddled to the American people, is based on a fairy tale.....a fraud....i.e., that "the market can provide anybody wanting a job, with a job"...

And Boehner, et al, fail to add to their grandiose claim: "IF" the market does well—this will create jobs—[i.e., no economist on Earth will say with certainty how the market will act in the future]—and yet, the Republicans state their claim as FACT—that is what makes it a fraud!

Further, this fraud is compounded when the Republican's true agenda is exposed: To justify cutting taxes for the 1%--PERIOD--i.e., to pander to the GREED of those who have bought and paid for their seat in Congress [the ugly underside of Citizens United]....

However, to cover-up their true agenda, the Republicans claim the 1% will then use this windfall of cash to build factories all across our fair land....and jobs will rain-down like moonbeams....and everyone will have a job in the corporation....

Yes, folks, it is a fairy tale....

Regarding the Republican cover-up, however: Been there, did that—it is called Supply-Side, or Neo-liberalism—and, in fact, rather than build factories all across America—they built factories in the Far East, and hid their profits in the Cayman Islands—and we learned that Neo-liberalism [the corrupt practice of siphoning America's wealth away from the consuming middle, and giving it to the 1%] has a shelf life of about 7 years before it sends the economy into meltdown—in 1987 & 2008—[a predictable result] cumulatively costing the American taxpayers trillions of dollars to prevent another Great Depression!

It, of course, would be better if we could refer to the Republican party, today, as the Grand Old Party— but it isn't---is has become a party without redeeming social value--and it has become a magnet for demagogues like Cruz and Cotton, et al— ideologues who pose more of a danger to Americans than ISIS....

And we need to start making the American people

aware of the Republican agenda, today.....the greatest enemy of democracy is ignorance—and democracy falls apart without an informed electorate....

Ref: OUR GREED AND IGNORANCE, Amazon/Kindle

Jim Green, Democrat opponent to Lamar Smith, Congress, 2000

CHAPTER SEVEN

President Obama/Council of Economic Advisers:

One of the most perplexing questions asked of Washington [hereafter DC], today, is: When "Fix Unemployment" was a mantra of the electorate in the 2008 election [before the meltdown]—Why did DC [inside the Beltway] turn its back on a solution?

DC will, of course, vehemently dispute the assertion raised by this question....but the question asks where is our Commission, etc., that is *specific* to end the insidious "social" problem: Unemployment?

Unemployment has the most dire "social" consequences of any problem facing America, today. It is the reason our youth are armed to the teeth, and killing each other at epidemic rates in every major city in America!

And the list of negatives from unemployment is almost endless....

When the mysterious new disease AIDS started killing Americans at record numbers—We, as a society, via the CDC, set out to find what was causing this dread disease—so we could create measures to prevent it....

But rather than using this model to create measures to prevent unemployment—DC instead harked back to the erroneous belief:

The market can provide "anybody wanting a job, with a job", and relied on anachronistic economic theory to create legislation, specifically HR 2847.

The result was a disaster—the 2010 election, as the electorate struck back with a vengeance because DC did not "Fix Unemployment"....

The truth is, the market has been unable to provide "anybody wanting a job, with a job"—since the mid-1970's—and "High and persistent unemployment has pervaded almost every OECD country since the mid-1970's" according to international economist [as well as every credible economist], Dr. William F. Mitchell.

Unemployment is an either/or proposition--And save for a lone legislator, Representative Conyers,

DC has been virtually indifferent to this proposition—and his legislation, deficit-neutral HR 870—has been treated as if were the plague….

Proposed here, like Social Security Insurance, is: The Neighbor-To-Neighbor Job Creation Act, a deficit-neutral, federally mandated Social Insurance, owned by our employed, to hire/train our unemployed. For a modest 4% of salary policy cost we can create more "private-sector" jobs in 6 months, than our current path [HR 2847], in 6 years.

The unemployed win, and capitalism wins…..

See: FULL EMPLOYMENT IS A PRO-MARKET CONCEPT, Amazon/Kindle

Jim Green, Democrat opponent to Lamar Smith, Congress, 2000
http://www.amazon.com/James-L.-Jim-Green/e/B001KHZIMM/ref=ntt_dp_epwbk_0

CHAPTER EIGHT

THE NEIGHBOR-TO-NEIGHBOR JOB CREATION ACT

[Hopper ready proposed legislation]

A Pro-Market, deficit-neutral, federally mandated, Social Insurance, owned by our employed, to provide a fund to hire/train our unemployed.

SECTION 1. SHORT TITLE.

This Act shall be cited as The Neighbor-To-Neighbor Job Creation Act [To establish employment/training opportunities for the unemployed in compliance with the "Legal Authorization" in Public Law 15 USC § 3101, for the creation of a "reservoir of public employees", anytime our unemployment rate exceeds "3%", with an emphasis on training for market needs, including a training stipend, where there is a shortage of trained workers--hereafter NTN].

SEC. 2. DEFINITIONS.

In this Act the following definitions apply:

(1) SECRETARY- The term `Secretary' means the Secretary of Labor.

(2) STATE- The term `State' has the meaning given such term in section 102(2) of the Housing and Community Development Act (42 U.S.C. 5302(2)).

(3) TRUST FUND- The term `Trust Fund' refers to the Department of Labor Full Employment Trust Fund.

(4) UNIT OF GENERAL LOCAL GOVERNMENT- The term `unit of general local government' has the meaning given such term in section 102(1) of the Housing and Community Development Act (42 U.S.C. 5302(1)).

(5) URBAN COUNTY- The term `urban county' has the meaning given such term in section 102(6) of the Housing and Community Development Act (42 U.S.C. 5302(6)).

(6) WEB SITE- The Secretary shall establish an Internet Web site to serve as an information clearinghouse for job training and employment opportunities funded by the Trust Fund.

SEC. 3. EMPLOYMENT OPPORTUNITY GRANTS TO STATES, LOCAL GOVERNMENT.

(a) Use of Funds-A recipient of a grant under this

section shall use the grant primarily for infrastructure repair, including, but not limited to:

> (A) The painting and repair of schools, community centers, and libraries.
> (B) The restoration and revitalization of abandoned and vacant properties to alleviate blight in distressed and foreclosure-affected areas of a unit of general local government.
> (C) The augmentation of staffing in Head Start, child care, and other early childhood education programs to promote school readiness and early literacy.
> (D) The renovation and enhancement of maintenance of parks, playgrounds, and other public spaces.

Respectfully Submitted,

Jim Green, Democrat candidate for Congress, Dist 21, TX, 2000

ADDENDUM:

Sec.4. IMPLEMENTATION REQUIREMENTS.

1] Based on the truism that we have far more

work to be done in America, than we have persons to fill these jobs....make work jobs is nonsensical....

2] Renewable funding is mandatory....this is not a "jump-start" solution—and is based on the BUFFER STOCK EMPLOYMENT MODEL—an expanding and contracting public workforce—that expands during a downturn in the market, and contracts as employees return to the private sector....

3] The funding is deficit-neutral.

CHAPTER NINE

COMMONS SENSE ECONOMICS

- We cannot siphon America's wealth away from the consuming middle without causing economic collapse—[1987 & 2008—i.e., Supply-Side Economics has a shelf-life of about 7 years before the economy collapses]--
- When every waking moment in capitalism is spent pondering ways to eliminate as many of us humans, as possible, from the workplace—to increase profits—why on earth would anyone rational look to this model to solve an unemployment crisis?
- Unemployment is a "social" problem—and "our government" has an absolute responsibility to step forward with a viable solution.
- We should never condemn the CEO who closes a plant when they are losing money—but we should be outraged by a government that is indifferent or incompetent in finding a viable solution to the resulting "social" problem caused by plant closings.
- Capitalism thrives when we have a robust, employed, consuming public—
- "Public-sector" jobs are an accelerate to

"private-sector" jobs—and HR 1000 will create more "private-sector" jobs in 6 months, than HR 2847 The HIRE Act, in 6 years, if ever—

- The belief that "public-sector" jobs can only be created by increasing the deficit, or equals a massive government program, such as WPA—is a belief that is suffering from a lack of imagination—
- The Humphrey-Hawkins Full Employment Act [hereafter H-H] which provides a "legal authorization" for the creation of a "reservoir of public employment" anytime our unemployment in America rises above "3%" is a Pro-Market solution—and is an *indispensable* tool for economic survival in a modern market economy—See also HR 1000 [currently in Committee]--
- In the mid-1970's—the colliding forces of automation, globalization, innovation, etc., reached a critical mass, resulting in ubiquitous unemployment—and has left our leaders conflicted—ever since—regarding what to do re the displaced employee—and given "automation" alone—fewer and fewer jobs are being created with each passing year in the 21st Century.
- Our response in America in the mid-1970's, was the passage of H-H, above, in 1978—but inexplicably this law has yet to be implemented—and the resulting high unemployment cost Carter his re-election in

1980--

- "Most [Americans think] that anybody willing to work should be able to find a job." per President Obama, in "The Audacity of Hope" – and a Zogby poll found 86% of Americans believe this--i.e., it is not the American people standing in the way of our implementing H-H—it is bad advice—
- The correlation between high unemployment and our sluggish recovery is absolute— A comprehensive public employment program, in compliance with H-H, such a HR 1000, or The proposed "Neighbor-To-Neighbor Job Creation Act": A federally mandated, Social Insurance, owned by America's employed--to provide a fund to hire/train our unemployed, or like program in compliance with H-H--*is the answer.* For a 4% of salary policy cost we can end our unemployment crisis in 6 months.
- a federally mandated, Social Insurance, owned by America's employed--to hire/train our unemployed is Pro-Market, and pro-the American people—a "win-win"—The American people win, and the market wins…..

Jim Green, Democrat candidate for Congress, 2000

CHAPTER TEN

President Obama/Council of Economic Advisers:

President Obama had a weapon during the Great Recession, not available to FDR—i.e., the $800 billion plus percolating up through our economy, annually, via Social Insurance claim payments i.e., from Social Security Insurance [which has reserves of $2.5 trillion in Treasury securities]—In short, but for these funds we would not be talking about having narrowly averted another Great Depression--we would be buried in one!

The lesson is: Social Insurance is a vital ingredient in building a vibrant and decent society—AND, Invent a better widget, sell the company for a million bucks, and retire in South Florida [capitalism]—is as well a vital ingredient in building a vibrant and decent society.

So why do we have this war of words pitting the two against each other—rather than educating the American people regarding the INDISPENSABLE symbiotic relationship they have to each other?

Further, the market thrives when we have a robust, employed, consuming workforce….i.e., unemployment is "no one wins" proposition---the jobless lose, and the market loses….and over the past 65 years we have had only one year in which our unemployment has dipped below 3%-- 1953…with 12% closer to our true rate, today, and 11 million still unemployed…..

And yet, we have the "legal authorization", on the books, to limit our unemployment to "3%" [15 USC § 3101—at NO time should our jobless rate exceed 3%], and given "automation", alone, an expanding and contracting public workforce is INDISPENSABLE to the EFFECTIVE functioning of a modern market economy—i.e., our economy going forward in the 21st Century….

In sum, a major source of the malaise that hangs over our recovery, today, in spite of our gains--is our failure to FIX UNEMPLOYMENT…and inexplicable given the above "legal authorization" limiting our jobless rate to "3%", in solving our unemployment crisis:

Proposed, here, is deficit-neutral THE NEIGHBOR-TO-NEIGHBOR JOB CREATION ACT [Amazon]: A federally mandated, Social Insurance, owned by our employed, to provide a fund to hire/train our unemployed. For a modest 4% of salary policy cost we can create more "private-sector" jobs in 6 months, than our current path, HR 2847, in 6 years.

Reference: HR 1000/FULL EMPLOYMENT IS A PRO-MARKET CONCEPT, Amazon

Jim Green, Democrat opponent to Lamar Smith, Congress, 2000

CHAPTER ELEVEN

I would like to take credit for this—but I can't—I found it posted on a blog—and would give credit if the author would come forward—it is what President Roosevelt meant by "All we have to fear, is fear itself", and it is gripping America, today, and sapping away our energy—and is the source of our entropy—and if we fail, this will be the reason….

"Conservatives are such cowards: they are afraid of gay people getting married or serving in the military; they are afraid of bringing terrorists to super max prisons in the US from which no one has ever escaped; they are afraid of the boy scouts letting gay kids in; they are afraid of everyone voting and are constantly suppressing the vote under some bogus voter fraud theory; they are afraid of letting students vote at their universities; they are afraid of women having the right to choose; they even are afraid of women getting contraception [the real issue actually is a women's agency and control over their bodies]; they are afraid of immigration reform leading to citizenship because they are afraid of-- name whatever reason; they are afraid of mandating gun purchasers to undergo background checks for crazy people and terrorists; they are afraid of people smoking pot; they are afraid of climate change being real and contradicting their beloved Bible; they are afraid of legitimate campaign reform; they are afraid of Muslims; they are afraid of blacks; they are afraid of atheists; they are afraid of hippies; they are afraid of socialists; they are probably still afraid of monsters under their beds; they are just rank cowards and keep making things up to be afraid of…..”

Anonymous

CHAPTER TWELVE

FAIL-SAFE ELECTRONIC VOTING

TO THE READER: Given you have gotten this far, and agree with the proposed changes—And particularly relevant given the radical extremists on our Court striking down a critical part of the Voting Rights Act, on 6/25/13, and Citizens United, putting our elections up for sale to the highest bidder—our democracy will be in peril unless, and until we have a "fail-safe" electronic voting system. The following is my proposed solution, and like every solution proposed, here, your feed-back/proposed improvement, etc. is welcomed:

THE FAIL-SAFE ELECTRONIC VOTING ACT

1) EVERY electronic voting machine (hereafter EVM), must be inexpensive, identical throughout the U.S. in a 1/150 ratio, and _must count and produce a hard-copy of the recorded votes_. In addition, an extra copy of their recorded votes would be produced (not necessarily a hard-copy), marked "Voter's Copy", and containing "NOTICE: Do Not Destroy Until Every Election On Your Ballot Is Certified". [If Wal-Mart handed

us a paper with "trust us" as a receipt for our purchases—*We would be outraged!* And yet that is our current electronic voting system—and this regards our democracy!].

2) *After confirming that their votes are recorded correctly*, the voter would then insert the hard-copy ballot into a software-free (count only) optical scanner (hereafter OS), for a second count. The hard-copy ballot would be retained by election officials in the event a candidate asks for a recount (*not possible under the current system, and which undermines the legality of each such election*). The EVM and the OS must be manufactured by different companies (which is universally true today).

3) Election officials assigned to oversee the EVM, would be prevented by law from overseeing the OS, and vice-versa, and stiff criminal penalties would be imposed for violations.

4) Further, every EVM would be programmed with raw data re the total registration rolls, by party, and norms for their voting history, etc.,----as an "alert" to a possible irregularity, such as an "Under-vote"—or "vote-flipping" etc., and *standards* established to suspend certification where there is an "improbable result", at least temporarily, of a particular election until the discrepancy is cleared up. (This is what computers

do best, and it would be very easy to create such a program).

5) At the end of the election day, tallies would be taken from the EVM and the OS, for each candidate. *If the tallies didn't balance for any given election, or if there is an "alert", that election cannot be certified until the "error" is corrected.* If the candidates agree (the victory is certain), minor discrepancies in the count could be disregarded. While probably rare, the Voter, or a random sample of Voters, would be required by law to return their Copy of the recorded votes to the election office to clear up any "error", or where an "alert" signals the need for same.

6) Further, every state provides for a recount when the total vote falls below a certain percent of difference between the candidates, impossible to conduct with the current EVM—and thus Congress must mandate the following regarding presidential candidates: A RUN-OFF election is mandated and triggered in those states where the percent of total vote is less than .5% of difference between any given candidates; said election to be held on the second Saturday following the election, on PAPER BALLOTS ONLY, and contain ONLY the names of the relevant candidates, for instance: "Barack Obama, Democrat" and "John McCain, Republican"—with oversight in counting by a representative(s) of each party—said procedure

providing more than adequate time to meet the Electoral College mandate. NOTE: Had this been the law in 2000, Al Gore would be our president, and the American economy would not be in meltdown!

7) Finally, absent the above safeguards, and until these safeguards are in place--Congress must mandate that PAPER BALLOTS, ONLY, can be used in our presidential elections. This is not a "partisan" issue, it is a "pro-democracy" issue. Most importantly, this will return the responsibility for our elections, and our vote counting, back into the hands of the individual voter, where it belongs, and out of the hands of "corporate control"---*it is after all "our democracy", itself, that is at risk if we don't take these steps---and in that regard, is there any time or cost differential that is too great?*

Reply To: Jim Green -- Democrat candidate for Congress, Dist 21, TX, 2000

CHAPTER THIRTEEN

President Obama/Council of Economic Advisers:

PRISON REFORM

The world economy underwent a paradigm shift in the mid-1970's, resulting from the colliding forces of automation, technology, globalization, etc., reaching a critical mass---And since the mid-1970's the Market has been unable to create the jobs necessary to its viability—With the result that "High and persistent unemployment has pervaded almost every OECD country since the mid-1970's." [Dr. William F. Mitchell].

Our choices in the U.S. were: Adapt and change our laws so that we could apply solutions that would effectively address this cosmic shift in the economy---Or, create a prison system [turn America into a Police State] so that we could hold in place our antiquated solutions....

We chose the latter, and by 1990 we had passed up every other country on earth in locking people up—

and currently we have 5% of the world's population, and 25% [one in four] of all prison inmates on Earth, in our prisons! We have the same number incarcerated as China, but they have a billion more people!

Further, by applying antiquated solutions during the Great Rescission, and rather than change—we currently have 25 million unemployed/under-employed Americans—and the CBO projecting it will be 2017 before we get back to even an anemic 5.5% jobless rate—and unemployment benefits long since expired!

The truth is, the world has changed, our solution to end unemployment hasn't, and the result has been a disaster [the 2010 election....].

Ironically, in 1978, the U.S. responded directly to the above economic shift in the mid-1970's, and President Carter signed into law 15 USC § 3101, which "authorizes" the creation of a "reservoir of public employees", anytime our jobless rate exceeded "3%"—a Pro-Market solution--the law was misunderstood, however, and to this day has never been implemented [and in spite of HR 870].

Missing in our current solution, and mind-set: Full

Employment is indispensable in creating a decent society, while Unemployment harms the individual, the market, and the larger society!

And accordingly, the path we should be on, and proposed, here, is a Pro-Market, deficit-neutral The Neighbor-To-Neighbor Job Creation Act: A federally mandated Social Insurance—owned by our employed to provide a fund to hire/train our unemployed. For a modest 4% of salary policy cost we can reduce our unemployment to 3% within a year of passage.

See also: ECONOMIC INCLUSIVISM, on Amazon/Kindle

Jim Green, Democrat opponent to Lamar Smith for Congress, 2000

CHAPTER FOURTEEN

President Obama/Council of Economic Advisers:

Unemployment is a "social" problem, we as a society, must solve—fix--

In "The Audacity of Hope" President Obama reported a pervasive mind-set on the part of the American people: "Most of them thought that anybody willing to work should be able to find a job….". A recent Zogby poll found that "86% of Americans" agree—

And as a democracy—it is not the American people standing in the way of this being a reality—the following is a framework for making it the law of the land:

If one is working--then they must chip in to help their neighbor get a job--and the vast majority of Americans ask: Why have you waited so long to ask us, Washington?

In creating "The Neighbor-To-Neighbor Job Creation Act" [hereafter NTN] it must contain the following:

1] It must be based on the premise that we have far more work that needs to be done in America—than we have persons to fill these jobs—[the notion that we would need "make work" jobs—is both a myth, and patently absurd]!

2] It must have renewable funding. This is NOT a "jump start" solution [such as HR 2847—HIRE Act]—i.e., funded until, in theory, the market will provide all the jobs we need [a fairy tale, at best, in any event]—

3] It will not add a dime to our deficit! Our unemployment is not the result of a lack of jobs, or money—but rather a lack of imagination—NTN is outlined, below.

4] It is based on the premise: Fix unemployment, and this will in turn fix the market—rather than the other way around—which is the flaw in our "conventional wisdom" today—and the reason why we still have 25 million unemployed, or underemployed, and a sluggish recovery. Also, disregarded is that if the market fails, the unemployed are out of luck!

5] NTN is a federally mandated, mutual

insurance—owned by our employed to provide a fund to hire/train our unemployed. And the infrastructure is already in place via FICA.

6] Using The Buffer Stock Employment Model—[an expanding and contracting public workforce—and an INDISPENSABLE component in a modern market economy]—NTN would be triggered anytime our unemployment exceeds 3%--and contract as employees return to the private sector.

7] For a modest policy cost of 4% of salary we can reduce our unemployment, within a year of passage, to 3%—and as "authorized" in Public Law 15 USC § 3101. For comprehensive detail see: www.Inclusivism.org –HR 870 [currently in Committee], and "OUR GREED AND IGNORANCE, on Amazon/Kindle

Jim Green, Democrat candidate for Congress, 2000

CHAPTER FIFTEEN

President Obama/Council of Economic Advisers:

It is a common scenario—tunnel vision—and frequently occurs in wrongful convictions—when the police or prosecutor are convinced they have the guilty party—and by closing their mind, convict the wrong person....too often the reason is government intractability—the inability to admit that a mistake has been made—and innocent people are being released almost daily, now, given DNA evidence.....

But this mind-set has broad application, and can be applied to many other situations....

For instance, the belief that "the market can provide anybody wanting a job, with a job."--it is patently false, and only ONCE since WW II has this method of job creation in America resulted in an unemployment rate below 3%--in 1953—and if we remove this belief from Boehner's grandiose claim that the Republicans are "job creators"--the entire Republican agenda collapses into a pile of dirt....

In the first scenario, as a result of this tunnel

vision—it almost always results in a gross injustice....and in the latter the injustice is perpetrated on the American people...86% of Americans believe that "anybody wanting to work should be able to find a job"--but we are not looking for a solution on behalf of the American people—because we believe we have the solution....

The larger question is: If we are committed to job creation in America [and we need to create 200,000 jobs monthly, just to keep up with the birthrate]—but our method for achieving this is wholly inadequate—how do we solve our pervasive unemployment problem—unquestionably the most pernicious "social" problem facing America, today?

America is a "can do" nation—if we had decided to put a lawn mower engine in the Saturn V rocket, in our spectacular trip to the moon—we would never have gotten there—a consummate metaphor for our current job creation methodology in America.

We can hardly blame the Democrats for celebrating our current 5.5% UE rate, given the vitriolic climate in Washington, as we inch downward—but.....

We have the solution at our fingertips—a "legal authorization" to limit our UE rate to "3%", tomorrow—at no time should our UE rate in America exceed 3%--but save for Congressman

Conyer's deficit-neutral HR 1000—implementing this Pro-Market solution has been obscured by tunnel vision.....IMHO

Ref: OUR GREED AND IGNORANCE

Jim Green, Democrat opponent to Lamar Smith, 2000

CHAPTER SIXTEEN

President Obama/Council of Economic Advisers:

TO solve our unemployment crisis, as we advance into the 21st Century—*we must* create a "reservoir of public employees"—as authorized in the "legal authorization" in 15 USC § 3101--with renewable funding paramount in our solution [i.e., we must abandon our "jump-start" mind-set].

It is a "win-win" solution—the jobless win, and the market wins...

At present, All of the OECD countries suffer from chronic high unemployment—and all are using the same methodology to create jobs:

They stand on one foot and then the other waiting on the market to create their jobs—

That is, job creation is intrinsically linked to the state of the market, and if the market fails—the unemployed are out of luck....

Unemployment is a "social" problem, with serious social consequences—but rather than being treated as a problem we as a society have the responsibility to solve—such as the cure for AIDS, or Polio—

Rather, we use a model making the solution contingent on an outside factor: The highly erratic nature of the market—with the empirical evidence, alone, offering consummate proof that we are on the wrong track—

In short, we do not have on the table, at present, *any* program specific to addressing/ending this extremely serious social problem—and we need to ask *why*?

Further, the problem is compounded by work being lost to "automation"—but rather than turning back the clock, we need to apply the maxim—We need to adapt and change in a world that is changing whether we like it or not….

Specifically, going forward we need to acknowledge that an expanding and contracting public workforce is an *indispensable* component to the *effective* functioning of a modern market economy.

And in the absence of this truism, at present, both the jobless, *and* the market loses....

Jim Green, Democrat opponent to Lamar Smith,

2000

CHAPTER SEVENTEEN

President Obama/Council of Economic Advisers:

THERE IS NO MORE IMPORTANT "RIGHT" IN AMERICA, TODAY, OR MORE IN DANGER—THAN THE RIGHTS OF THE AMERICAN EMPLOYEE

The Koch brothers, and those of like mind in the plutocracy/oligarchy [hereafter P/O] prefer employees in America to be without "rights", over profits....

Since WW II they have spent hundreds of millions of dollars buying legislators, governors and legislatures to cement "at will" employment in every state [only Montana limits "at will" to probationary employees]--and on March 9, 2015, in Wisconsin, the P/O reached the half-way mark [state 25] in their calculated effort to destroy "employee rights" for workers in Wisconsin, and to destroy the union movement in America—and the stated goal of their Republican minions in Congress is to duplicate the Wisconsin law in all 50 states.

The theory of the P/O, of course, is quite simple--

less money for those who work in America, means more money for us—in short, the motive is PURE GREED! And the P/O have committed a billion dollars, given the worst Decision in SCUS history--Citizens United, to buy the presidency in the 2016 election.

The over-arching result of the P/O buying politicians [not limited to the U.S.] who will cut their taxes [they prefer not paying any], and destroying the rights of employees, what Dr. William Mitchell defines as "ideological hegemony" in what appears to be a world-wide austerity mind-set—a starve our way to recovery mentality...the etiology for the austerity is because the P/O don't want to pay any taxes...

President Obama summed up the alternative course when he said "There is no contradiction between making public investments and being a firm believer in free markets."

To change course we need to change the dialogue ....Unemployment is a *No One Wins*--the jobless lose, civility loses, and the market loses, to wit:

THE LAW OF DIMINISHED INCOME TO THE MARKET FROM UNEMPLOYMENT [hereafter the D/UE LAW]

Short Definition:

3% is the zero-sum threshold above which unemployment starts substantially undermining the Market--and the loss in income to the Market is compounded exponentially with each percentage point of increase in unemployment, above 3%.

Ref: FULL EMPLOYMENT IS A PRO-MARKET CONCEPT, Amazon

Jim Green, Democrat opponent to Lamar Smith, Congress, 2000

CHAPTER EIGHTEEN

Congressman Conyers.....we are clearly on the same sheet of music...my method to get there is slightly different and perhaps a blend of the two would provide comprehensive funding....my path for funding is similar to our current Social Security Insurance—and a system is already in place for collection—Specifically, [Google] deficit-neutral "The Neighbor-To-Neighbor Job Creation Act": A federally mandated Social Insurance, owned by our employed, to provide a fund to hire/train our unemployed. For one, the 1% will not be able to attack by their taxes going up—albeit a tiny fraction on stock transactions should be above that nonsense....a point that has yet to get into the national dialogue re unemployment is the adverse impact unemployment has on the market, to wit:

THE LAW OF DIMINISHED INCOME TO THE MARKET FROM UNEMPLOYMENT [hereafter the D/UE LAW]

Short Definition:

3% is the zero-sum threshold above which unemployment   starts substantially undermining the Market--and the loss in income to the Market is compounded exponentially with each percentage point of increase in unemployment, above 3%.

In short, HR 1000, etc., are PRO-MARKET solutions—a point that has been lost in the discussion.

A final point, we are reported to have 8,800 pending infrastructure jobs, alone, and legitimate grants to any jurisdiction, so requesting would appear to be in order, and within the framework:

- We have far more work that needs to be done in America, than we have persons to fill these jobs [the "make-work" mantra is nonsense].
- It must have renewable funding— "jump start" funding until the market kicks in [HR 2847] doesn't work—For one, the data shows the market is incapable, now, of creating enough jobs, and given "automation", alone, will create fewer and fewer jobs, going forward in the 21st Century.

- It will not add a dime to our deficit. Our unemployment is not the result of a lack of jobs, or money—but rather a lack of imagination—

With highest regards,

Jim Green, Democrat opponent to Lamar Smith, 2000

CHAPTER NINETEEN

President Obama/Council of Economic Advisers:

According to Webster's--a lie is a statement that is not in conformity with truth, or fact, specifically.....

We can't seem to give up the lie in America that "the market can provide anybody wanting a job, with a job"--in spite of it being patently false, and it becomes a fraud—given the Republican agenda....

For instance, with this belief, singularly, driving our job creation policies in America—only once since WW II has this resulted in an unemployment rate below 3%--in 1953---and a truism under this policy is that if the market fails—the jobless are out of luck [with 2008-9 as Exhibit One]!

So to reverse engineer this—let's take two circumstances....every politician since the beginning of the republic has promised good jobs for everyone, if elected...i.e., it is a given that "work" is a high priority for Americans—indeed, 86% of Americans believe "anybody wanting to work should be able to find a job."

Secondly, our current method for job creation is incapable of creating enough jobs......even at the "official" rate of 5.5%, we still have almost 9 million jobless as we inch downward [and given "automation", alone, fewer and fewer jobs are being created going forward]—the question is: What steps do we need to take to meet the will of the American people?

It is a "What works?" question....

Obviously there are other influences that come into play—but the only question, here, is:

With Jobs the #1 priority for Americans, and our current method for job creation incapable of creating enough jobs— How do we fix this?

And the irony is that we have a "legal" fix that makes America truly "exceptional"--nowhere else in the OECD do they have this law, and 10% UE is common in the Eurozone, 25% in Greece and Spain—specifically, 15 U.S. Code § 3101 with a "legal authorization" to limit our UE rate to "3%", tomorrow--i.e., at no time should our UE rate in America exceed 3%--

Unemployment is a *No One Wins*, the jobless lose, civility loses, and the market loses....but, aside from the persistence of Congressman Conyers—i.e., deficit-neutral HR 1000, etc.—this obvious solution to our unemployment crisis might as well not exist....

Ref: FULL EMPLOYMENT IS A PRO-MARKET CONCEPT, and THE NEIGHBOR-TO-NEIGHBOR JOB CREATION ACT [hereafter NTN], Amazon

Jim Green, Democrat opponent to Lamar Smith, 2000

CHAPTER TWENTY

Published in the Seguin Gazette, April 19, 2015

I see where George Rodriguez [Gazette 4/17/15] is still trying to peddle that the Republican party, today, is on the side of the rank-and-file Texan, and particular Hispanic Texans.

The Republican party, today, represent the Koch brothers, and like kind—they don't have the back of ANY rank and file who live in Texas, or anywhere else in America.

Here is a quick example: The Democrats have improved the lives of millions of seniors in America, via Social Security Insurance—and yet, the current Republican controlled congress already have legislation to destroy this program—albeit, the 1% don't pay a dime for Social Security [their tiny cost is absorbed in their sales]--

Note, the Republican party "today"--more on this shortly....

Also, note that Social Security is an "Insurance"-- one must work and pay in to file a claim.

Regarding the Republican party "today"--a quick test: Which U.S. president expanded Social Security to include working Americans who have become disabled? The answer folks, is Eisenhower—a Republican—

And at a time when the Republican party put the American people first—in fact, it never even occurred to Republicans then to destroy Social Security—why would anyone in their right mind want to!

Consider a couple of points: But for the $800 billion plus in Social Security benefit moneys percolating up through our economy after the 2008 meltdown [no thanks to Bush]—we would be buried in another Great Depression, today--i.e., it is also an indispensable economic benefit--

Also, but for the $2.7 trillion the government distributes back into our economy [our Defense, corporate welfare, etc.]--capitalism in America would fold in a NY Second! Yes, folks, we are a blended economy—thanks to the Democrats--and we are ALL the better for it!

A closing note on why the 1% should pay more in taxes, and would not pay ANY taxes if they could get away with it—they earned their great wealth from us, folks, and this creates a fiduciary obligation to create a good and decent society for the people who gave them their wealth! But is anyone foolish enough to think they would do it voluntarily?

The Republican party today is controlled by a handful of GREED-DRIVEN, who buy politicians who will cut their taxes, and at the expense of the rest of us! PERIOD

The Republican party, today, has NO OTHER AGENDA—and anyone in the rank-and-file who think the Republican party, today, has your back-- is not paying attention.

The lesson is: It is up to the rank-and-file who vote Republican to get your party to represent YOU— are you up to the task?

Jim Green, Democrat candidate for Congress, Dist 21, TX, 2000

CHAPTER TWENTY-ONE

[I couldn't resist including this—because it is the source of so much misery in the world…and yes I am the author…..]

A MESSAGE FROM GOD

MANY CENTURIES AGO, a man of the cloth, we don't know his name, and in a flash of insight (perhaps induced by peyote) told his flock that "sex is a sin". And lo and behold he learned that by taking a very natural and healthy part of our life and turning it into something that was "dirty and nasty", that he could imprison his flock, and fill his coffers, and hallelujah it was a great day for the Lord!

Quickly, his miracle spread to other churches in his village, and then to the next village, and then the next county, and then state, and soon it spread to all the churches in the ancient world, and all of their flocks cowed in fear and shame and became imprisoned, and their coffers over-floweth. Hallelujah, it was a great day for the Lord!

And to keep the myth alive they started

inventing stories, half-baked stories, that made no sense to anyone who is rational, such as "Mary was a virgin"—well, she just had to be a virgin because she would never partake in anything that was dirty and nasty, like sex (if you're doing it right), and this was necessary to make "sex is a sin" make sense...so they invented a Mary that was "sinless"--you get the picture. And their coffers over-floweth. Hallelujah, it was a great day for the Lord!

No one seemed to be bothered that when we play tricks on the human mind by taking something that is very natural and healthy, such as sex, and make it dirty and nasty that all kinds of bad things happen to the human mind:

Such as most pedophiles, and most serial killers, and voting Republican, and unwarranted suicides, and most mental illness, and unwanted pregnancies. (Teens not wanting to have sex is the perversion, not the other way around, and by replacing sex education and condoms, with unrealistic "abstinence", and by using blather about "low self-esteem" to shame them into not "sinning"—We have a teen pregnancy in the U.S. twice that of England and Canada!).

But none of this mattered, because their coffers over-floweth, and Hallelujah, it is a great day for the Lord!

There is a cure--------Tell the right-wing loonies who want to ruin your life to shove it....Amen....

GOD

A BRIEF ADDENDUM: When the U.S. Supreme Court denied certiorari—where the violation of my constitutional rights were obvious, and criminal negligence on the part of the government defendants in the death of our son, equally obvious—[detailed in THE HARVARD BOYS CLUB, Amazon/Kindle]--I filed a Petition for Rehearing [which is automatic]—and included the following. The Clerk of the U.S. Supreme Court called me at my work in California, and asked that I withdraw the "cartoon" [a reprint from The NEW YORKER] from my Petition. I refused on the basis of the First Amendment, and it remains in the archives at the U.S. Supreme Court [Docket #: 79-1627], to this day. The wording [not that clear] is: "Excellent, excellent. A fine blend of truths, half-truths, and blatant falsehoods".

IN THE

Supreme Court of the United States

October Term, 1979

No. 79-1627

JAMES L. GREEN,

Petitioner,

vs.

OTHER BOOKS BY THIS AUTHOR ON AMAZON/KINDLE/BN:

- **THE HARVARD BOYS CLUB:** Hitler's Assault On Our Freedoms From His Grave

- **MY LETTERS TO PRESIDENT OBAMA:** Confessions Of A Compulsive Letter Writer

- **OUR GREED AND IGNORANCE:** Poses A Far Greater Threat To America, Than Terrorism

- **LETTERS ON STEROIDS:** Confessions Of A Compulsive Letter-To-The-Editor Writer

- **THE FIRST TIME I HAD SEX:** And, The Religious Intolerance Attack On America

- **WHY PRESIDENT OBAMA LOST THE 2012 ELECTION:** A Wake-Up Call

- **ECONOMIC INCLUSIVISM:** Neo-Capitalism/An Anthology: Inclusive pro-market solutions to our social problems

- **AMERICA IS ONE SICK MF:** Why Greed-Driven America Went Off The Rails....

- **EVERY GIVEN SUNDAY:** A Scientific Formula To Predict NFL Games

- **IT IS IMPOSSIBLE TO BE A CHRISTIAN,**

AND VOTE REPUBLICAN

And others: http://www.amazon.com/James-L.-Jim-Green/e/B001KHZIMM/ref=ntt_dp_epwbk_0